Above the water of my sorrows

Above the water
of my sorrows

**PONGO TEEN WRITING
FROM
KING COUNTY
JUVENILE DETENTION**

EXECUTIVE DIRECTOR
Richard Gold

ASSISTANT DIRECTOR
Eli Hastings

PROJECT LEADERS
Emily Holt, Vanessa Hooper

WRITING MENTORS
Carol Thompson, Emily Caris,
Erin McCormick, Fred Nollan, Liz Koontz,
Lynn Zhao, Mark Johnson, Ron Rivard

PONGO PUBLISHING
Seattle, WA, December 2015

Published in December 2015, by

PONGO PUBLISHING, INC.
PMB 308
4701 S.W. Admiral Way
Seattle, WA 98116
www.pongoteenwriting.org
info@pongoteenwriting.org

Publisher: RICHARD GOLD
Designer: CELESTE ERICSSON
Editor: EMILY HOLT

PHOTO / IMAGE CREDITS
Cover and pages 1, 23, 49, 55: *Life Vest*
Copyright © iStock.com / Floortje

Cover: *Carribean Water Surface*
Copyright © iStock.com / Grafissimo

Printed and bound in the United States of America.

Dedicated to all of the Pongo teen writers.

Thanks to the following grantors for their generous support of the Pongo Teen Writing Project and this publication:

MICROSOFT ALUMNI FOUNDATION · SEATTLE7WRITERS
CITY OF SEATTLE, OFFICE OF ARTS & CULTURAL AFFAIRS
SEATTLE FOUNDATION GIVETOGETHER: ARTS ENGAGEMENT
IBIS FOUNDATION OF ARIZONA · ONEFAMILY FOUNDATION
FALES FOUNDATION TRUST · THE NORCLIFFE FOUNDATION
GLASER FOUNDATION · JEFFRIS WOOD FOUNDATION
MOCASSIN LAKE FOUNDATION · LUCKY SEVEN FOUNDATION
SOCIAL VENTURE KIDS · SEATTLE FOUNDATION YOUTH GRANT
TELLUMIND FOUNDATION

CONTENTS

Preface x

LIFE IS A DREAM WITH NO BED

AIMAN   Family *2*

DANIKA   Dear Mom *3*

THOMAS   My Dad *4*

ADELE   Happy Birthday *6*

HAKIM   We Came from Saudi Arabia *8*

SAVANNAH   Why Are You Blue? *10*

EVA   My Best Friend Was Murdered *11*

DARRIUS   When My Brother Got Shot *12*

DYLAN   Brother and Sister *13*

TRINITY   Nothing Will Bring Me Down *14*

TOBY   The Days I Miss *16*

CAREY   Good Day | Bad Day *17*

OMAR   Metal on Metal *18*

JADA   The Thunder Is in the Past *19*

CELIA   Coyote Ridge (Correction Center) *20*

GABRIEL   I'm Making a Moving Poem *21*

WOUNDED HEALER

ALEX   My Whole World Stopped *24*

BELLA   Unwanted *25*

KATELYN   Dear Mom *26*

GRACE   The Nightmare That Never Ended *28*

NICOLA   If Meth Wasn't in My Life *30*

KAHLIL   144 Ways *32*

LILY   Just Lay It Out *33*

TREY Memories *34*

PETER My Spaceship *36*

KELSEY Stepdad *37*

IMAN My Life Story *38*

XAVIER If God Were Looking at My Life *40*

ROSA Missing My Family *41*

MIGUEL Family *42*

BRYSON Freedom *43*

IVANA GrizzlyLifeJacketTornadoDandelion *44*

MAX Amazing Amanda *46*

KIARA Wounded Healer *47*

BLUE RAGE, BLUE FIRE

COURTNEY Me as a Hermit *50*

JAMIE Abandoned *51*

COURTNEY Finally Opening Doors *52*

KAYLA My Brother *53*

CHASE Anger *54*

ANTONIA Adia'Zalika *55*

LENA Longing for Another Life *56*

BRANDON Not My Real Sandals *58*

AMELIA Do You Really Know Me? *60*

OWEN Capitol Hill in Seattle *62*

DAVION Physical Love *64*

ANISA Really Buttery Popcorn *66*

ETHAN   Something Missing   *67*

JUSTIN   Me and My Board   *68*

IRIS   A Gaining Loss   *70*

SELENA   Para Mi Mamá y Mi Papá   *72*

DOMINIC   Independent   *73*

THAT MISSING PUZZLE PIECE

AIDAN   The Abusive Father   *76*

MAKENA   Being Mixed   *77*

KIRRA   Black Hole   *78*

MATIAS   The Story of a Cell   *80*

TYRONE   Cops   *81*

JUDE   People Fall   *82*

TONESHA   Dear Dad   *83*

CLYDE   How It Feels to Be Trapped   *84*

PEYTON   Calm   *85*

NAYELI   Am I Me?   *86*

JACKSON   Memories of Danny Fresh   *88*

MIKA'IL   I'm Locked Up   *90*

SARIM   Fighting with IF   *91*

OCTAVIA   Clarity, Happiness & Love   *92*

JEWEL   I'm a Diamond   *94*

AMATA   For You   *96*

SEAN   How I'm Feeling   *97*

DINAH   The Missing Puzzle Piece   *98*

Preface

The young writers represented in this volume are our teachers. Through their poetry they bravely illuminate the complicated legacy of childhood abuse and neglect, for themselves and for us. As human beings, especially as children, we often adapt to personal trauma by feeling that it is our own fault. We can persecute ourselves endlessly in private torment.

More hopefully, the young people also teach us that writing in response to trauma can be transformative. After opening up their tender hearts on the page, the youth see the world differently, with less sense of personal defectiveness and shame. In fact, they experience joy in the writing process—finding insight, perspective, relief, and purpose in poetry.

Welcome to Pongo Teen Writing. Pongo has collected surveys from 1,000 of its writers from detention and elsewhere, which show that 100% enjoyed writing (though 35% were new to poetry), 98% were proud of their work, 94% expected to write more in the future, 82% felt better after writing, and 75% wrote about things they normally didn't discuss.

This book celebrates the writers. It also celebrates the 20th anniversary of Pongo Teen Writing, of which I'm proud to be the founder. Pongo is a volunteer-based nonprofit that mentors personal writing by youth inside sites such as juvenile detention centers, homeless shelters, and psychiatric hospitals. Pongo has worked directly with over 7,000 youth.

The 68 poems in this volume are samples of about 900 poems that were facilitated by Pongo at King County juvenile detention in Seattle from fall 2011 to spring 2015. The authors' names and some details in their poetry have been changed to protect their identities.

In addition to the teen poetry, Pongo wants to share its method with you. We offer trainings and presentations around the country, to teach our techniques for facilitating therapeutic poetry. I have also written a book, *Writing with At-Risk Youth: The Pongo Teen Writing Method* (Rowman & Littlefield Education, 2014). We hope that you will visit the Pongo web site, where youth can use Pongo activities to write online, and where teachers and counselors can download Pongo activities and also read about Pongo's teaching approach and techniques. There are hundreds of teen poems for inspiration, as well as a blog. Our web site is *pongoteenwriting.org*. Please contact us at *pongo_publishing@hotmail.com*.

Finally, I would like to acknowledge the many people who make Pongo's work possible. I thank our friends at King County juvenile detention, including Pam Jones (director), Karen Kinch (volunteer coordinator), and Lynn Valdez (supervisor). I thank our friends at Seattle Public Schools inside detention, including teacher Stacy Vida. I thank our friends at King County Library inside detention, including librarian Jill Morrison.

I thank our funders, who are listed on the dedication page. I thank Pongo's talented leaders and wonderful mentors, who are listed on the title page. And lastly, I thank our authors, who move us, inspire us, and teach us every day.

SCHOOL YEAR **2011-2012**

Life Is a Dream with No Bed

Family

The ones we have
end up burning our life,
losing our trust, for the
worst of it. Life is
a dream with no bed. The
steps we take every day
make the past look like
hell. And this family bond I have
is hard to break. This
family is like a blood vessel running
through my body. Once it's broken
death is my only choice.
Family is a power we have.
If we don't use it, the
punishment we go through will
never be forgotten. My blood
vessel will run through
me until Death comes for
me. The ones we love
are family. The ones we trust
are family. The ones we live with
are family. Life without family
is like a remote without a TV.
You press the buttons, but
don't see the vision.

Dear Mom

I just thought you should know that life is hard—
I've seen a lot: *murders, love like grandma's peanut butter*
pancakes, hate like my parents' addiction and absence,
my siblings tormenting me because I have a different dad
(theirs sent money, mine disappeared).

I'm loud, but it's a mask.
On the inside I'm quiet,
but I'm making sure I'm seen *and* heard.

I just thought you should know that your actions
make me hate you, everything you made me see—
it made me think you didn't care: *taking me to drug houses,*
letting people do what they wanted to me so you could score.

I'm going to be more than you were.
I'm going to make you proud of me.

I just thought you should know that I love you
and that the pain that you caused taught me a lesson
about how to treat my children: *I'll never do to them*
what you did to me.

I'm going to help them succeed.

My Dad

My dad was in my life
A normal person
No drug addiction
Just an alcohol problem
Before

Then it got crazy
Bipolar disorder
Beat the hell out of me
Talking about things that aren't true

Last I saw him
Was on a bus
He didn't even notice me
Like a stranger
Then he really saw me
And started to cry

I remember when his drug dealer
Came to the house
Asking me for money
I just snapped—
"Get the f#%& out of here!"
And my dad was like—
"What are you doing, he's my friend!"
Felt like I was teaching a little kid
That friends like that aren't friends

Then he just disappeared
Haven't seen him for two years
And now I'm on the same path
Waiting for him again

Happy Birthday

Happy birthday
To me
Yeah, I guess, me

Summertime is here
My dog is here
My little Rhenish chicken is here
Mom sleeping in the sun
I run out in the field
Free, so free
Nothing can happen
The sun falling asleep
Mom rising for what I thought was me
She puts on a movie
She sits on a chair
I sit on the couch
Her boyfriend right next to me
I fall asleep
Body intertwined with the couch

Realizing with that
I'm intertwined with her boyfriend
Mom's gone
Why is he here?
I bump him to wake him
He starts bumping back
I stop suddenly, maybe he will leave
Soon his troll-like hand goes to my waist
I hit him in the face

A few nights later
He takes me from myself
So for my birthday I got:
My mom's boyfriend and

A now forever distant mother

We Came from Saudi Arabia

We came from Saudi Arabia
But my dad wouldn't help my mom.
He didn't help get food.
He came and went as he wanted.
He would hit my mom.
He had another wife on the side.
My mom told him, "Step up and be a man."
He left and ended up in jail.
I was 5, I didn't know what was going on.
I don't want to be like my dad when I grow up.
It's the worst feeling I could have,
Seeing him hit her,
Not knowing when he would be home.

Now that I'm older
I started getting in trouble with the law.
Now I'm stressed.

I wish I could go back and fix this,
But there is only the future.
I keep going back to what I know,
Hustling, selling drugs, all of that.
All this keeps bringing me back in here.
Now I want to turn that around.
Now I'll go to school,
Staying away from drugs,
And then I'll have money.
When I don't drink and smoke,
I have money,
I go to the skate park,
Because I love to skate.
I need to stay away
From those who are there dealing.
It's hard to turn around,
To hang with the right crew.

Why Are You Blue?

Why are you blue?
Wake up, please pull through.
Things happen so fast.
Jayson, do CPR.
Call 911.
Go outside, help Annie.
Ambulance arrives.
Thinking: I'm never
Doing heroin.

Face all one color,
Eyes glazed over.
The thought:
She's dead.

Shocked.
Scared.
Feel to cry, but couldn't.
Matthew holding me
While we talk to the police.
Mad.

———

Dedicated to M.

My Best Friend Was Murdered

The last time I saw Althea
was her body at her funeral.
She was always there for me,
bringing me food, buying me clothes.
She was my second mother.
I was 10, and she was just 23.
We were walking with
her boyfriend, my brother, a friend
when someone drove by.
We were just talking and walking,
the five of us.
Then shots rang out,
her boyfriend yelled, "Get down!"
When I got up, Althea was shot.
She was bleeding severely.
They took her to the hospital.
She died there.
I didn't see her die.
The last thing she said to me
was about what did I want.
Then she was gone.
At 12 I learned
not to let people get close
because they might also get shot.
Might also leave.
Might also break my heart.

When My Brother Got Shot

My past,
When my brother got shot,
I was mad and sad all at the same time.
I didn't even know what to do.
I was hurt.
I didn't speak for two weeks.
I became an angry person.
I wouldn't listen to anybody,
Wouldn't talk to anybody.
Only person I'd talk to was my brother.
Ended up messing up my probation,
Left my group home,
Searching for weeks
For the dude that shot my brother.
Still been looking.
I'm still tore up inside about that.
And it doesn't help,
The fact that I've never had my parents in my life.
Always had my grandma, though.
When things went wrong I'd go to her for help.
I've been in and out of jail.
I have nightmares of my brother getting killed.
That's why I call him every day to make sure he's all right.
My brother's my best friend.
I don't know what I'd do if I lost him.

———

Dedicated to my brother

Brother and Sister

We fought
We bickered

I hated her
She hated me

Blinded by our problems…

Mom and Dad split up
There's no food in the fridge
We're getting evicted
Our brother just got locked up

Then it hit us…

She's my blood
I'm her blood

That's my sister
I'm her brother

We've only got each other

Nothing Will Bring Me Down

When I got raped
I was sad
It makes me feel like crying
Never telling the police
Refusing to testify
I feel like an empty abyss
I feel like I could've cried a river
I cried forever
I went to sleep and hoped it has all been a dream
I felt that if I had sex with a guy I actually liked
The feeling of being raped would go away
But it didn't
If I could ask him something
I'd ask *Why me?*
Why me of all the other girls in the world?
There were so many that would've went willingly
Why me?
I'd ask
Did he actually know me?
I never saw his face

It didn't matter to me
I put it in a box
I sent it down a river
And I hope it never comes back
I feel like this will make me stronger
Most of the kids who go through bad stuff
Will be able to help other kids when they get older
I'll be able to know what it is like
And tell them when I was 12 I got raped
I've been in detention seven times
I know what it's like to have parents who don't want you
I did it
I made it out
And I did something with my life
Nothing will bring me down

———

Dedicated to S.

The Days I Miss

I miss the days when me and my family
Were a happy family
I miss the days when me and my family
Used to go to Seafair
Watch the Blue Angels
I miss the days when me and my family
Spent time in the living room
Watching TV
I miss the days when me and my family used to argue
Because I knew they still cared
And now we don't argue
We just have meaningless conversations
Or sometimes just awkward talks
Because we don't know how to talk
To each other

Good Day | Bad Day

A good day is when you are given sincere smiles
and compliments, on your inside self, not just the out.

A bad day is when you lose your most important fan,
your loved one, or your pride.

A good day is when you hear the happiness in people
because it surrounds you with joy.

A bad day is when you don't know what the next day
will bring, and where you're going to end up.

A good day is when you are full of laughter, positivity,
and love.

A bad day is when you get too much negativity,
when everyone seems to want you to fail.

A good day is when you fail, but you have the same
hunger to keep trying.

A bad day is when you fail, and you hadn't tried at all.

A good day is when you can be honest, and be yourself
with someone you just met.

A bad day is when you have to lie about everything to
someone, and later on you begin to regret.

Metal on Metal

This isn't the way I planned my life to go.
I've been here far too many times,
Walked these halls far too many steps.
I am a caged lion.
I want to roar out my rage,
At these bars, at this cage,
At the chains upon my freedom,
At the separation from those I love.
My heart wants to never come back here,
To find a path around these doors.
I want that path where no one dictates
What I should do, when I should do it.
If I could get along with my probation officer,
If I could make my way through school,
Maybe I would not hear these doors again,
Metal on metal barring my way.
Maybe I would not hear these doors again,
And I could be someplace else, far away.

The Thunder Is in the Past

There are only attorneys on weekdays
And I got put in on a Friday

New Year's means times for changes:
Good grades in algebra
Mom and daughter communication
Cardio-respiratory workout
To get my heart pumping more

If I had a bonfire on New Year's Eve
I'd throw juvie into it
I'd throw trust in people I haven't truly known
I'd burn the day I ran away from my home
And my statements of hatred

When the fire burned out and the smoke cleared
There would be only gray ashes
That crumble when you touch them
Or fly away when you blow them from your fingers

Coyote Ridge (Correction Center)

There's so much…
Stress and missing my dad
Missing my mom and my sisters
School's been on my mind

But mainly…

I think about how I'm not going to see my dad till I'm 35
That's *20 years*
He's gonna miss out on my kids
My high school graduation
My college graduation—
Growing up

He just had a kid—my little sister—she's only 1
My other little sisters are 9 and 6…

20 years

Coyote Ridge is as far away as the sky

I'm Making a Moving Poem

I'm making a moving poem
This poem is not about happy endings
It ain't about survival
Or strife or making it out of the tunnel
This poem ain't about getting over
Your disease of addiction and depression
It's not about how you move on
From your old ways
This poem is not about forgiving the people you love
Who betrayed, abused, or misused you
It's not about walking into the sunshine
And into a new beginning
It's not about how you come a long way
From an ignorant child
It's not about heroes
It's not about serenity
It's not about courage
And it's not about enlightenment
No, this poem is not about that
You see this poem is not about you
This poem is not about you
This poem is not about you
This poem is not about you
This poem is not about you

———

Dedicated to the world

SCHOOL YEAR **2012-2013**

Wounded Healer

My Whole World Stopped

My whole world stopped

The gun went off
And reality slipped away

His body just lay there
Lifeless
No soul in him

The thought of death
It is a weird concept to grasp

He was only 15
And he committed suicide
Or was it an accident?
I don't know

But what I do know is
He is dead and gone

The life of my best friend is gone—
I wonder if he even knows he existed

Well, we all die eventually
So does it really matter?

———

Dedicated to J.B.

Unwanted

An empty baseball stadium,
littered with broken glass, beer cans,
pill bottles left from the group you went there with.

An old book that's been on the shelf
for so long, collecting dust.
It's a book about family.

Sand in the middle of the desert
during the day. You're dehydrated,
can't find anywhere, anyone.
You're isolated.

The quiet ringing in your ear
when you're sitting in your lonely cell.

Reaching out for something,
but never being able to grab it.

Dear Mom

I just thought you should know what I'm doing now.
I'm addicted to drugs and in juvie a lot. I am an unloved
person who spends a lot of time doing drugs to feel better
and not abandoned.

I just thought you should know how I'm feeling. I just
hate you. I hate my dad, too. I hate you because you left
me one night when I was 7 and never came back. The
police broke down the door to take me to foster care. But
even before that you brought home men who hurt me
and did bad things to me. I hate you for pimping me out.
I hate you for packing my nose full of white powder,
which is why I have breathing problems now. I hate you
for getting me into drugs. I hate you because I ended up
in a gang. I hate you.

I just thought you should know what I've been through.
Since the last time I saw you I've been in more foster
homes than I can count, but 45-50% of them were
abusive. I always ran, but the system found me, didn't
believe me, and put me in another, and another. The time
that I was going to be adopted was especially important.
They came and picked me, and I lived in their house for a
week before they found out about my history and they
sent me back.

I just thought you should know what I wish for the future. I hope that somehow I can yell at you without having to see you, to blame all this crap on you. Though it would do nothing for me, at least I wouldn't have to hold it inside any longer.

I just thought you should know what I don't miss about you...I don't miss you at all. I'm glad I don't have to worry about you leaving me again and not coming back.

I just thought you should know that there is nothing at all that I miss about you.

I just thought you should know that no matter what, you'll always be my mom, and I'll always love you.

———

Dedicated to my mom

The Nightmare That Never Ended

Meth addiction took over my life
I would get forty or fifty dollars from a jugg real quick
And bring it back to my home girl
I was still 12
She would go upstairs to the dope dealer
She would bring it back down, load it in the pipe
After it was all gone
I'd go out again
I'd walk two blocks from the hotel
And a man would pick me up
I was 12
It wouldn't end
It wouldn't end
Somewhere in there I overdosed
While I was getting a tattoo on my back
That says "Love is a Battlefield"
I don't remember when
The only time I was clean
Was when I went to juvenile hall
I was there for seven days
And then back to the same addiction
I would run away from the foster home
I'd go on North First Street in Yakima
Selling myself
To supply my drugs

And that's where my life began
That's when I became involved with the Norteños
A La Raza gang
I was 13
I had no family at that point
And the gang was my comfort
My safety
My home
I was walking on the wrong side of Yakima
By myself
I seen some Sureños
And I ran
They shot me twice in my left leg
I was thinkin' nothing of it
Got stabbed in my right leg
In the same moment
I didn't even feel it at first
I didn't even know it until I got home
That's when I realized I had to change
But I was addicted to my lifestyle
Knowing that I was gonna end up dead
I decided I wanted to live past 13

———

Dedicated to my parents

If Meth Wasn't in My Life

If Meth wasn't in my life I'd be beautiful
    Like a blooming, red rose.
If Meth wasn't in my life I'd feel free
    Like a queen.
If Meth wasn't in my life I'd feel happy
    Like when I'm on the basketball court.

But now that Meth is in my life I feel horrible
    Like the little kid I was without my parents.
Now that Meth is in my life I feel unhappy
    Like when a loved one dies.
Now that Meth is in my life I feel dead
    Like an incomplete puzzle.

The first hit made all my emotions go away.
I felt happy, on the top of the world.
I felt like the boss, no one could demand me
To do anything.

My next hit brought me away from my problems.
Everyone seemed happy because
I was happy.
I was on drugs because of everyone else.
I couldn't be successful
Without Meth.
I was a nobody
Without Meth.

My last hit took my breath away.
Unstoppable, like I could run a million miles
From my emotions
From the nightmares.
Didn't have to sleep
When I didn't want to sleep.
In a dream, where bad news
Wasn't real news.
Didn't have to believe,
Didn't have to listen.

———

Dedicated to R.E. and A.C.

144 Ways

If my eyes could speak,
They would tell you what I seen
In my life.

I seen a lot at a young age,
Before Seattle, down in Fresno,
Most ghetto-est place you ever been.
But it's normal for me.
I seen females getting slapped by pimps.
I seen people getting put into closets
So that others could smoke stuff
You don't want to smoke.

Mostly I seen gangs
Taking interest in people,
Stabbed for being in the wrong side of town
In the wrong colors.

My hood now, Tukwila,
Is a lot like Fresno.
It's active anyway you could put it.
People out there for money,
Doing anything for money,
A money freeway always with traffic,
Money any way you can get it.

I seen 144 ways to get
It.

Just Lay It Out

I am addicted
> to heroin, the devil's blood, and the sharp swords that
> open the way for it. My life is as painful and miserable
> as the fires of hell, and I am glad to feel high like the
> clouds, far above real.

I am addicted
> to feeling nothing and yet like I matter. I hate to feel
> the low of the high, of dealing with no feelings. The real
> me disappears like crystal smoke. Like a waterfall,
> the cloud drops, spreads, and is gone.

I am addicted
> to avoiding my brother's death and the outcome. I am
> trying to un-know things about myself. Betrayal comes
> in the form of a boy spitting game in my ear, using me
> as a bridge to his next OK place. His words have no
> weight, they float away. I struggle to see a way out, but
> the only one I know of is when I close my eyes before
> God and confess my sins and offer my trust.

I am addicted
> to the lifestyle of dancing with the devil, of wrong
> tasting so good. I am hiding from the future of the real
> me, which was just a road with no one stopping to offer
> me a ride. I am in a constant battle with myself.

I am addicted.

Memories

I remember when I got shot
I was 10 years old
I remember I was sweating
My heart was beating fast
I was afraid I was gonna die

My blood was leaking fast
Down my small arms

The gun was kinda big
The shot rang in my ears
With a big boom

I thought about my mom
I wanted her
And she was on the news
By my side when I went to the hospital

It changed my life
I think it turned me to a maniac
I started carrying guns at all times
I was never by myself
I stayed with a group
I was ready to ride
I was ready to shoot

'Cause if anybody ran up
I was gonna do the do

Until this day
I still feel like a maniac
In my brain
I don't know the way to act
Though I feel like I can change

———

Dedicated to my mom

My Spaceship

Sleepless nights
Like I am on a rocking ship
Flying through the solar system
Upside down, right side up
Chilling in a spaceship
The walls melt
And the days are endless
It feels like I am in a labyrinth of time and space
I feel trapped with no way of escaping
Sleepless nights because of my mania
My eyebrows are stuck up
Because my eyes won't blink
My skin feels like wax
Touching my hands, my fingers stick like plaque
My whole face feels numb
I try to close my eyes, but they are stuck open
Constantly jolting up
That is my bipolar

———

Dedicated to myself and family

Stepdad

Hurt, everyday
Abused mentally & emotionally
Drugs, alcohol daily
Weed, spice, you name it—I've done it
I looked on the brighter side
But darkness follows me

Why does he do this to me?
"Why me?"

I hate him, but he's my daddy
Fighting daily
Mom and Poppa screaming
"It's just a loud argument," she says,
To keep the kids calm

BAM! Right to the face
I drop to my knees, crying
"Why me?"
"Why does he do this to my family?"
I can't take this any longer!

On the streets, alone, homeless, helpless
"Why me?"
'Cause I chose this:

Now locked up with no family contact
"Why did I do this to *my* family?"

My Life Story

I was a little boy
when my mom and dad passed away, in Africa.
Both parents were soldiers,
to protect their family and their country.
Life in Africa was hard, with the family trying to survive.

When I was little,
I saw both parents get shot in front of me in my house.
I was like 5 or 3.
When I saw that, when I felt both my parents get shot,
I almost had a heart attack.

Seeing that kind of stuff
made me feel like there's no world.

Losing both of my parents was like losing half of myself.
Until this day, I keep thinking about
my mom and my dad.
I wish they were here to teach me how to be a man,
to keep me out of this place.

I've been through a lot of stuff:
good times with my friends,
and also bad stuff.
When my friend told me to join a gang, I almost did.

I learned a lot of stuff too:
I learned some stuff
from my older sister and my godmother.
I learned some stuff from my counselors and teachers.

I dedicate this story to the kids that got no family.
Keep your head up no matter what.
Take care of your family, whoever is around.
The right thing is to keep going to school, play a sport,
stay off the street.
I know life is hard without a mom and dad there
to teach you what is wrong and what is right.

Be the only strongest survivor out there.

———

In memory of my mom and dad

If God Were Looking at My Life

He'd wonder why I made the choices I made—
joining gangs.

He'd understand that my childhood wasn't good,
that what I experienced was being raised in the hood.

He'd know the way things had gone for me—they've gone
outrageously horrible in this jail of addictions.

He'd remember how things went when I was very little,
like seeing my cousins in the streets and my uncles
suffering as their children destroyed their lives.

He'd know that I was a good kid at first.

He'd know that I'm trying to change certain things,
like my attitudes towards people. See, I was taught
to hate most of society, that nobody cares about you
but your family.

He'd know how hard it is to change because craziness
runs through my veins.

He'd want me to understand that life is a movie
I'm tired of seeing.

If God opened a new door for me, it would lead me
to peace. I don't know what it looks like.

Missing My Family

Today is a typical day: boring, and going to school.
But a couple things are different.
I'm in a place of solitude, away from everyone,
and silent, as usual.
A lot of new people, a lot of new faces.
But there are a few that I miss the most.
My family.

We're a little chaotic, and tend to go insane sometimes.
If someone were to see us, they'd see us as disoriented.
It's kind of like when you shake a snow globe,
there's always a little clump of snow
that sticks to the side of the glass and doesn't move.
That's my family.
But that's what makes us family.

My family are some of the loudest people on our block.
The neighbors hear us screaming about silly things,
like an old doll getting stuck in a tree.
It's been stuck there for like four or five years now,
even through the Washington windstorms.

My family has communication issues sometimes,
but we always have each other's back,
and we will never let each other down.

One saying in our family is: "You don't have to like the
person, but you do have to love them. They're family."

Family

This is my second year spending my birthday in here,
but I look at it as just another day.

I'm mainly worried about my family.
In November 2010, my parents got taken away
by immigration,
and I was in here.
If it happens once, you just think the worse.

My friend snitched me out in court
and snitched my parents out, too.
It was early in the morning, my dad went to start the car,
and they grabbed him and took him inside in handcuffs
to do the same to my mom,
right in front of my 6- and 7-year-old sisters.

My brother brought my sisters in to visit me.
They were crying, didn't know when they'd see
their mom and dad again.

If there were one thing I wish for my little sisters
it would be to finish school and have their parents
by their side.

If there were one thing I wish for myself
it would be to get off the wrong path

and meet them on the right one.

Freedom

I'm gonna jump up and down when I'm outta this place
I'll go have some of Grandma's turkey with cherry flavor
   —This is not just a plain turkey, it's got juice in it

Then I'll go mud bogging with my friends
in the forest behind the elementary school,
maybe bounce up on a few trees
My friend Dexter can hit at least 60 mph on his bike,
do donuts, and take turns so sharp the tires skid out

I'll pick up my girl on my bike
and take her to the movies at Southcenter to see *Ted*
And then we'll rent the second *Ghost Rider*
from the Redbox, get some popcorn, Pringles,
Reese's Pieces, Cheetos, Doritos
Then head back to the living room
to kick back in front of the 84-inch TV

Outside you can choose to share your name
In here you have to wear a bracelet with it

Freedom tastes like licorice
Freedom smells like the beginning of winter
Freedom sounds like cars rushing by you
Freedom feels like the wind blowing through my hair
and against my face
Freedom looks like rain falling

GrizzlyLifeJacketTornadoDandelion

I hope that someday I can be as strong as my mother.
My mother is as strong as a bull
ramming into its next opponent.

My mother is always ready to recover from the past
and look forward to the future.
The past has been one of a refugee, mother of seven,
abandoned by her husband, no schooling.
With every reason to give up, she didn't.

She has always been my backbone,
always there when my world was as empty as a well.

She keeps my head above the water of my own sorrows,
like a life jacket.

My mom can be as strong as a tornado,
sucking in everyone's troubles and making them
seem small compared to what she went through,
setting the troubles down
as destroyed as an old building.

Pay attention to my mother's lessons.
She can see into the future.

If I could go back
I would listen to all her warnings and lectures
that I didn't think would help.
My mother can be strong in ways you don't expect.

She can be as strong as a dandelion
breaking through the sidewalk,
and when I talk with her
she blows all my sorrows away like spores,
making me believe I can also break the cement.

My mother's strength can be gentle.

She can be as gentle as a grizzly bear with her young—
quick to scare away predators
but even quicker to comfort.

If I could change one thing,
I would be the wind to the dandelion,
carrying away her sorrows.

———

Dedicated to my mother

Amazing Amanda

This one time when I had a really bad counseling session, we went on a really long walk. For two hours, we just walked around the golf course she lived by. We talked about why I was upset, she told me how much she cared about me, how much she wanted me to do better.

I had only been there for three weeks, but I felt at home after that walk. I never thought I would feel at home again when I went into foster care. I thought it would be the worst three years of my life.

I remember after that walk, lying in bed thinking, "How could someone who just met me care about me so much?" She reminded me of my mom.

After the walk I remember thinking about my future, how maybe I wouldn't have to be alone. I was thinking I might have someone at my high school graduation, at my college graduation, someone who will care about me for my whole life.

I only lived at her house for three months, but even if I stay at a facility for the rest of the time I'm in foster care, it would have been worth it to have those three months.

I don't think I've told her any of this. I'm not really good at talking about my feelings or what I'm thinking about. I wish every foster parent could be like Amanda.

Wounded Healer

You see that I assault others
and burn my arm with lighters
You see that I break down in church
and don't believe in God's help
But you don't know me

You would know me if...
You knew how hard it was to not be able
to see your brothers, sister, or your mom
You knew how I felt about
being in treatment for nine months:
punished, abandoned, forgotten
You knew what it's like to live in an environment
where everyone is racist
But you don't know me

You see that I am not in my right mind,
that I'm staring at something else
You see that I use narcotics to soothe myself,
to take myself away from all this
But you don't try to help me
But you don't know me

You would know me if...
You knew how I cry every night
because I feel like no one cares
You knew how I tried to commit suicide
You knew how I dream of becoming a healer

SCHOOL YEAR **2013-2014**

Blue Rage, Blue Fire

Me as a Hermit

I feel like hiding in a shell like a little hermit crab.
I'd have long claws
And little antennae.
My claws carry all of my negative feelings.
When I'm scared they crunch into a little bundle.
Hiding from pain.
Hiding from disappointment.
Hiding from reality.
If I was a crab I would want to live in a little terrarium
Because all the terrariums are all the same.
Nothing bad would happen.
Except running out of food and water.
But my owner would give me food,
And he would hold me with love and care.
Hopefully.
Living on the beach with all those scary predators
And scary humans would be too much.
I would probably have a little hermit crab breakdown.
I would probably go drown myself in the ocean.

Abandoned

Sometimes I don't feel emotions,
kinda like the anger I have is left behind.
I'm feeling half-dead.
I'm being pushed out of my family,
but I'm also being drawn back in.
I'm in here because
my mom was picking me up by my ear,
and I pushed her back, so she called the cops.
She doesn't want me home.
I'm going to be in a group home.
And that's when I start to feel like I just don't care,
and my emotions go away.
Before my emotions go away,
I feel raged, mad, sad,
and then I feel reality.

There's a bird
and when it's sick,
the mother of the animal
pushes it out of its nest
so it can fall to its death.

Right now,
I feel like that bird that's fallen
and about to hit the ground.

Finally Opening Doors

Most of the time I'm latching locks on doors.
I'm afraid of all the emotion coming out.
I'm afraid of judgment.
I've afraid of showing my emotions.
I feel like they win if they see my emotion.
One time I was at my house.
I live with my grandparents upstairs
'Cause my mom was abusive.
I would make it a point to never let her see me cry.
My mom would get a look on her face
Like she accomplished something.
My mom lives in the basement.
Once you walk through that door
You get this feeling of anger.
Something bad is going to happen.
It's a place I don't like to be.
Especially with my mom in there.
It ended up her trying to drag me out of the basement
By my ankle.
My grandparents were like, "Stop! Stop!"
As soon as she saw me crying she stopped
And just went downstairs.
I felt defeated.

———

Dedicated to my future

My Brother

Since I was 8 he molested me.
It's always bugging me.
If I could, I would ask him why he did it,
why he made me feel it was okay.
I want to tell him it made me feel gross.
He made me feel like a slut
'cause he would always call me those names,
then he would tell me he was sorry
and that I was beautiful.
I would ask him what went through his mind,
what made him think of it,
why couldn't he just leave me alone when I asked him to.
I felt disgusting when I looked in the mirror.
I didn't think I was pretty.
I just want him to think of me as a sister
and nothing more.

Anger

When I think about anger, I think about being in jail.
My anger is like a gun, ready to pop off at any moment.
My anger sounds like tires screeching on the road,
because the anger is driving the car.
My anger looks like blue rage, blue fire.
My anger smells like gunpowder,
after the gun has been fired.
My anger feels like being in a coma.
I don't know what I'm doing.
I can't feel anything.

Adia'Zalika

Her name is Adia'Zalika.
I wanted to keep her.
Her father didn't want her.
He named her.
He named her, and he did not want her.
She's watching over us.
I feel like if she was here I don't know
If things would necessarily be different.
Half of me doesn't want her here.
I don't want her to be at home while her mom's in jail.
She would already be able to walk and crawl.
I feel that being older, having a career and a husband,
I feel that's motherly love.
Half of me wants her here.
I don't know if that makes me a bad person.
'Cause the reason I want her here is for selfish reasons.
'Cause I want to be loved and love her.
But God is a better parent than I could ever be.
And knowing the struggles that I'm going through now,
They would just affect her.
I don't want her to end up like me.
Instead of being Adia'Zalika,
The little girl whose mom's in jail,
She's Adia'Zalika, the princess in heaven.

Longing for Another Life

If I could I would escape
to a world I imagine every night
when I try to go to sleep
or daydream.

It's another world,
different from ours.

It's like an Alice-in-Wonderland world,
completely the opposite from here,
something you'd want to go to.

The colors are brighter, more colorful,
colors you couldn't think of.
You could do magic.
You could make candy appear out of air.
You could make sparklers with your hands.

In this world I'm not lost.
There would be puppies,
a Cheshire cat, a lot of penguins.
Animals can't talk, but you can understand them.

The only hard thing about this world is
if you do anybody wrong,
you get sucked up into a black hole
and disappear into thin air,
and you're sent back from this world.

Being sent back from this other world
would be like detention,
like your whole world was once full of colors,
and now it's just black and white.

In this other world, you could be
whoever you want to be.
If you wanted to be famous,
you could be famous.
If you wanted long hair,
you could have long hair.
People wouldn't put you down.
This world doesn't have pollution,
always clean air, and the sun is always
shining, even when it rains.
The moon is always full.

You can work if you want to,
but you don't have to.
Everything is paid for.
The government doesn't want you to have to labor.
Everything is done.
You get to relax.

When you go to sleep there,
since everything you'd ever want is already there,
your dreams are reality,
it's so vivid.

Not My Real Sandals

I haven't gone out there in a long time.
I don't understand why everyone here
has to wear the same clothes.
I suppose they want to make everyone feel the same.

I haven't stepped on real dirt for a long time.
Just yesterday, a lot of people here began to pick on me.
Someone bounced the ball off the wall
and hit me in the head on purpose.
It makes me feel homesick.

I haven't gone out there in a long time.
I hate the isolation from the rest of the world.
I've had it at home.
My dad works graveyard.
When he's sleeping, I come home from school,
and my stepmom's working.
There's a lock on my door so I won't go out.

I haven't gone out there in a long time.
Sometimes I don't care.
I don't mind being in there.
I have things to do.
At home,
my little brother stomps on the ground,
and I get annoyed.
Now I miss it.

I haven't gone out there in a long time.
My little brother saw me get cuffed.
He couldn't get over it
until he heard my voice on the phone.
I didn't get to say goodbye to him.

I haven't gone out there in a long time.
My real mom died.
I feel like any other person would:
sad, angry, too much all at once,
all bundled up inside me.
I think I could have done something about it.
It was a drug overdose.
I could have stopped her.
That made me act out.

I haven't gone out there in a long time.
My crime was arson.
The only way they knew it was me was from
the matches in my pocket.
I'm at a behavioral school.
I have a problem with authority.

So I end up isolated,
sleeping under a blurry window
behind these huge metal doors
I can't get through.

Do You Really Know Me?

I laugh a joyous laugh
I smile every day
I stare a glossy stare
You think everything's okay
but do you really know me?

I struggle with the hurt
    I hide it behind a smile
I fake these positive thoughts
When really I'm suicidal

My eyes show no emotion
But they're crying for you to stop
I tell you I don't judge you
    but the pain you bring me
can't be covered up

You're changing fast
    I'm changing fast
And it's all because of ADDICTION

We're hiding what we feel inside
our problems causing more friction
I'm tired of holding myself back
You think I'm fine in this lifestyle?
Then do you really know me?

I'm not saying I'm ready for change
and I know you're not either
We've dug ourselves our own graves
and we keep getting weaker

We think this addiction makes us strong
We think we're in control
But I think we both know
life has more to hold

We follow the lies we tell ourselves
to get us through each day

When you're ready to know
yourself (and who you can
become) let me know

Do you really know me?
　　No, you really don't
I'll show you someday
　　But right now I'm stuck on Dope

———

Dedicated to PorkChop

Capitol Hill in Seattle

When you think of Capitol Hill what do you think of?
It's a lot darker than you think
Meth grows on trees
As the city sleeps they reign their terror
Smashing car windows on the streets
There is a group of people
A group of meth addicts
That car hop
Some of them blap windows
Some of them steal cars
Some steal bikes
Some of them boost
Some of them forge
Capitol Hill is a black hole
A rotating black hole
It makes you or breaks you
I never see anyone leave
They might take a break but they always come back
Unless it's to jail, death,
Or luck out and find a sugar momma
When all you know is crime, drugs, and repeat
And then donuts because that's what you live on
Then the black hole is all you know

Jail
Crime
Getting high
Back to jail
And a sentence
I don't see a way out for me
I've been doing heroin for three years
I started shooting up meth just to up the ante
To the point of insanity
I'm not trying to lose my mind
It's already lost
The only way out is to have someone die on you
To have death change you

———

Dedicated to B. and P.

Physical Love

When I was little, my mom wasn't financially able to take care of me, but she was always there physically, making sure that I got on the bus to school, making sure I was keeping my hygiene up.

When I got into my early teens, I started dealing drugs. It would do me good one moment, then the next it would do me bad, get me sent to juvenile.

My father was there for me financially, but not physically. He always lived two states away. Besides, when I took it upon myself to get on the Greyhound to go see him, I would never see him at all. Instead of paying child support, he would send me money on the first of the month. He would send me something at Christmas. I loved him for the financial love he gave me, but I felt he abandoned me physically.

It led me to do a lot of bad things in my life.

I lived with my mom until I was 13 or 14, then I moved in with my aunt 'cause my mom kinda flew off the edge. I think it was because she was trying to do it all herself, raising three kids to be independent. I was kinda a parent before my daughter was even born, taking care of my little sister.

There was a time when my mom wouldn't come home for weeks. There were things about being a kid that I missed out on. It was pretty much me and my sister after a while 'cause my older sister left. In some ways I'm angry at my mom for doing that. In some ways I'm happy she did that because it made me independent.

I feel if you are a child yourself you shouldn't have to raise another child, but it did help me as far as raising my child today.

Really Buttery Popcorn

I miss the homemade rice that my mom makes for me.
She makes it for me when I am sick.
I miss lying in bed with her and watching scary movies.
We'd make a bunch of popcorn, really buttery popcorn.

I miss coming home from school
and my mom asking if I needed help with homework
or if I want to help with dinner.

I miss my mom because she is always there for me
if I need someone to talk to.
Me and my mom are really close.
She is such a strong woman.
She has been through a lot.

When she was my age, her mother abandoned her.
She was in foster care,
had to share almost everything with my uncle.
She has always tried her hardest
to keep a roof over our heads,
to give as much love and kisses as she could
to me and my sister.

It's hard to say everything when there's so much to say.
I appreciate her more than she knows,
even if I don't show it all the time.
I just want my mom to know
I love her bigger than space.

Something Missing

Wrestling.
I can't wait to get out and start wrestling again.
My adrenaline starts pumping, I get in the zone.
When I wrestle, I don't remember much,
I just black out. I just zone everything out.
It's like nothing matters, you're just right there.

I'm focused on his body movements,
Which leg he's leading with, what openings he has.
I'm focused on his arms, his stance. I focus on circling.
If you stay in one place, that's stalling.
You have to circle around your opponent.
When I see an opening,
I shoot for a double-leg takedown.
If he's trying to, like, hook on the back of my neck,
I can snap down.

Wrestling is like anger release.
When I'm mad at something, or someone,
I take it out on wrestling.

Now, it feels like I'm out of shape.
All we do here is, like, run around.
There's not much physical stuff, like sports.

It's like there's something missing.
It's like you lost your phone,
And you can't get on Facebook.

My and My Board

Every day is being on constant guard,
not knowing what's gonna happen next.
It's like walking around a corner
and getting hit in the face with a baseball bat.

One time when I was 11 years old,
I got cereal without asking,
and I got hit on the back of the head
and dropped to the floor.

Saying a bad word,
sometimes I slipped up my words,
and I got whipped by a belt.
It was like a real-life Cinderella story.
I had a list of chores every day—
Windexing, cleaning dishes,
cleaning bathrooms every two days.
If there was a hair on the floor,
if it wasn't to a perfect T,
I'd get hit or yelled at.

During the night,
I'd go to the skate park
when no one was there.
It really shows how they cared about me.

Skating was the only thing I ever did
besides cleaning.
It didn't make sense to me.

I wondered why my parents acted the way they did.
These are people that love you.
Getting screamed at in the face,
trying to back up into a wall,
you want to scream,
your little mind is trying to flee.

I got away,
found a loving family that treated me with kindness,
and didn't attack me when I made faults.
It was the family I always wanted,
I always pictured.
My mom had motherly love.
My stepdad and I would play baseball,
pick up a skateboard 'cause I skated.
They were there for me
when my dad and stepmom never were.

Now, I feel freedom from this dysfunction.
I always wanted to get away.
I grew up lonely.
Me and my skateboard,
that was my only friend.

A Gaining Loss

Before, I was only thinking about myself.
When I ended up seeing a positive pregnancy,
I had to think about that child's life.
And it made me think of all the lives
I have done wrong to in the past.
I didn't want to ruin this child's life.
I have hurt so many people
And associated myself in the wrong circles.
I didn't want my child to see their mother
As a cold-hearted person,
I just wanted to give the child the best life
I possibly could.
And being only 16,
I knew I could only give half of that.

I kind of felt like a plant,
Like a flower,
With no nutrients,
Feeling lost and stuck in a dark cave.

When I found out I lost that baby,
I felt like I had been crushed by a boulder.

It made me think about the father,
It made me realize I didn't want to have a family
With someone like him.
I realized I didn't even trust him.
It reminded me of Snow White.
At first she trusted the lady with the apple,
But instead she was sitting on a throne of lies.
I thought I needed this baby to have a purpose in life,
But with all these things coming to the surface
I am seeing so many opportunities for myself.
There are so many possibilities
And aspects I have never explored,
So many things I know I can fulfill in life
That I had never thought of before.
It feels a little overwhelming.
I never really thought of myself as being able
To be anything,
Just thought I would end up being a typical housewife,
Stuck at home cleaning up after people.
I have hope in myself now.
I have purpose.
And I know I can be someone.

———

Dedicated to my family

Para Mi Mamá y Mi Papá

Why did you leave my brothers and sisters and I? Why did you think drugs were more important than taking care of your kids? Why would you call when you didn't want to talk to me? Why would you make me drink beer and dance for you when I was only 8 years old? Why did you have to beat us so brutally?

Even though you weren't the best parents, I still love you unconditionally. I wish that you would have taught me better than to do drugs and run away, commit crime, end up in jail like you. I think about you every day.

Mom, why did you risk doing drugs when my little brother was inside you?

Dad, why would you make me smoke weed with you? Why would you let mom beat me more than any of the other ones? Why would you leave us alone with Mommy if you knew she wasn't stable enough? I think about you every day.

I'm angry like I've been hurt too much. I'm sad like I've been left to teach myself. There's only one way I can take it, by doing the things I do.

I wish that you wouldn't have done drugs. Now that you are gone, that's how I feel close to you.

Independent

My mom was in the bedroom
As I entered the messy bedroom
She was lying on her bed
I knew something was wrong
I ran up to her
I said, "Mom, Mom!"
I shook her, and she didn't wake up
I yelled for my dad
"Something's wrong. I think she's overdosing!"
He helped me drag her into the bathroom
And sprayed water on her
I started shaking her
She came-to and faintly said
"What's wrong, what's wrong?"
She said, "I'm okay," and nodded off
Tears just came to my eyes
And that's when I left my house
My dad took care of her after that
I'm alone since I was 14
I remember at first
It made me wish there was someone I did love
But after a while I just became independent
I didn't think about anybody else

That Missing Puzzle Piece

The Abusive Father

The very first time I saw my dad
it wasn't a very good time,
but at least I got to see my dad.

I was at my stepmom's house,
and it wasn't very pleasant.
My dad was drunk,
and he was cooking
some breakfast for me
and my little brother.

He said *What the f*** are you doing?*
I was playing with the glass china action figures.

He picked up hot grease from the frying pan
and boom—
I flew far out the window
and hit tar.
There's a scar on the back of my head.
It wasn't very pleasant.

The dog was licking my face.
At the end,
at least it showed
that an animal cared for me.

————

Dedicated to J.

Being Mixed

I'm not accepted by my family.
I'm judged for being only half and half.
I have never felt fully accepted
by my father's family or my mother's family.
I always feel like an outsider.

People think it's a blessing to be mixed,
but sometimes it can be a curse.
Words can hurt like a bullet in the heart—
words like *half-breed, too dark.*

My dad's side—they're Ethiopian church-going,
kind of fanatics.
My mom's side—we're not religious.
They put me down for not being religious, being a sinner,
not being able to speak my native tongue.
It isn't my fault. My father has never been in my life
to be able to teach me.

I always wanted to fit in,
not feel like the black sheep of the family.
I want them to tell me they love me,
rather than making me feel like an outsider,
out of place, never comfortable.
Sometimes I feel ashamed to be only half,
but it's not like I was asked to be born.

I just want the feeling of being mixed to be beautiful.

Black Hole

I would paint myself in black and white.
I don't see my life in color.
I would be black,
and the background would be white.
I would paint myself black
because I feel like a black hole.
I feel like a black hole because
somebody says something to me
and it's in my head.
I can't get it out.
A black hole feels full.
Full of everything.
It's always gonna feel full,
but it's never going to be full.
No matter how many people say it's full,
it's just not full.
My head is the black hole.
Someone will say something to me,
and I'll be like, "Leave."
But it won't leave.

It will stay, and it will get louder.
It will stand out more.
Other people can just take it and throw it away.
They're all empty.
They're always gonna be empty.
No matter what they do.
My heart feels empty.
My soul.
Sometimes I feel like I don't even have a soul.
No feelings.
No thoughts.
Immortal.
Like a zombie.

———

Dedicated to my mom

The Story of a Cell

You can tell how many times it's been repainted,
see who's been there by all the tagging.
It gets cold in the night
and hot in the day.
Under the beds you can tell there's been bloody messes,
fights, horrors.
They have a savage side.
The spiders and the flies fighting.

You can't really get a lot from a cell.

The courtroom cells are like their cousins.
You can tell how many different group members
have been in there.
I saw one date that was from '85.
The doors are wood with wire screens.

Cops

Some mean some nice
He had his knee stabbing my spine
    Cops
Some mean some nice
I got caught with drugs, and he let me go despite
the disrespect I showed him that night
    Cops
Some mean some nice
I stole some spray paint, and he held out his nine
    Cops
Some mean some nice

——

Dedicated to all the homies in jail and dead

People Fall

I'm from a street where people struggle
to stand on both of their feet.
My mom and my dad have always tried to
take care of me,
but they can't even take care of themselves.
People fall like leaves from a tree.
My mom, she tries so hard, but
she doesn't even have enough money to get by.
I don't know where I'm from.
I'm native, and I don't even know my native culture.
I don't even know who my mom is personally, or my dad.
I don't even know my family.
I'd like to know if they're still there for me.
Only time I see my mom is when I'm in court.
I can't even talk to her.
I know my tribe.
But nothing else.
I don't know who to talk to.
I've never met anyone from my tribes.
They're all on the reservation, in different states.

Dear Dad

I just thought you should know
That I'm strong without you.
I'm strong as a young tree.
New leaves grow out of my branches.
I just thought you should know
That you hurt me 'cause you're not here.
You're here, but you don't act like it.
You have too many kids.
I want you to spend time with me,
But you think money will buy my love.
When I think of you, I think of money.
You are an old money tree,
Money all over the tree,
With girls hanging over the branches.
Your bark is hard and mean and old.
I just thought you should know what I've been through.
Since the last time I saw you I have grown
'Cause my mom helped me.
But both parents should be there to help you grow.
My mom taught me to never depend on a man
Because of you.
Basically, you are an example.
You are not reliable.
My mom is a strong, independent, beautiful,
Reliable, caring, all-the-good-stuff kind of tree.
Even though you try to buy my love,
My mom will always be my mom
'Cause she's actually here taking care of me.

How It Feels to Be Trapped

There are things they can do in here with your freedom.
They'll let you know what it's like to have fresh air,
but you can't actually be free.
They let you know how the air feels,
but then you have to let it go.
It plays with your freedom.
It makes you think about what you done to get in here
and what you could do to get out.
At the end of the day
there's not nothing you can do.

When I'm able to touch the air,
it takes me to the front of my house.
It's called home,
where you have the most freedom,
playing football in the front yard,
running the ball,
juking friends and family,
and eating orange chicken after.

When you're trapped inside,
it makes you feel like you're nothing.
No air at all.

Calm

I'm from a street where
it's full of apartments
and bumping roads
and beat-down mailboxes.
I see dogs inside the fences
of houses.
There are pit bulls barking.

Crickets everywhere,
Chirp, chirp, chirp.

Woodpeckers in the trees.
I hear them pecking at the wood.

I am looking out the window
at everything.

I am calm
like an alligator.

Am I Me?

I'm the happy one when I'm with my family.
I like to go out to church with them.
When we are holding hands and doing a prayer
In the center of the church, I'm happy.
There are stained-glass windows
And a lot of religious statues.
I'm not very religious.
I just go because of my family.

I'm the hyper, crazy one when I'm out with my friends.
I am the one in the park
Upside-down on the monkey bars.
I am the one in the car on the freeway
With my hands out the sunroof.
I am the helpless one who can't change being who I am.
And I am the one who likes fashion.

I am the one in the long-sleeve shirt
With a jean vest.
I am the one in ripped jeans with low-heeled boots.

And a hat.

I am the messed up one who thinks
No one is better than me.

I am the one who fights.
I am the one who does stuff wrong,
On purpose.

I am the hurt one when I can't see my loved ones,
And I am in juvie.
I am the one who's nothing.
I am helpful to staff,
But I don't always do as told.

I am the strong one who is determined to move on
And become something in life.
When I sleep, I am the dreamer
Who imagines a different life.
I imagine me when I wasn't a gang member.
I was an innocent little girl,
Doing and living for everyone else,
Not for myself.

I am the one with the tattoos, but they are not me.
And one day their meaning will be
Bigger than what they are supposed to be.

———

Dedicated to my family & my soulmate

Memories of Danny Fresh

What he did for me before he passed away—
he was my older brother.
Wasn't blood or anything,
but that was my older brother.

He did a lot for my mom, too.
My mom was out of town in Atlanta,
and I had gotten shot in my leg four times.
He came to the hospital with me.
I told him not to tell my mom,
and he never did.

He was one of those guys that I looked up to.
For him to die the way he did—
it's just f***** man.

I'll never be the same.
Got no one to talk to anymore.
Got no one's house to run away to anymore.
It's like half of me is gone,
and the other half of me is trying to hold on
to the memories, every day.

He had that old school swag,
Adidas with the saggy sweats and a basketball jersey.
Never wore a snap back,
always wore beanies,
always always always.

Really tall,
as dark as dark can be,
darker than that keyboard.
That was Dan.
He taught me how to drive.
I miss my brother.
I close my eyes, I see my brother.
I miss my brother.

My palms got sweaty,
like they are now.
My heart started racing.
Every time I blinked,
it felt like there were enough tears to fill a cup.
I couldn't move.
All I could think about
was that last hour
I spent with my brother.
I miss Dan.
I miss Dan.

Ain't gonna ever be another happy day.
Maybe the day my son is born.
I'd name him Dan.
Daniel Isaiah Tyler.

———

Dedicated to my brother Dan

I'm Locked Up

I'm locked up in a jail cell, and I can't get no bail,
and I'm thinking about the dreams
and the life that I've failed,
and I'm still in this place called America,
walking up on these people that are pale.
It feels like a walking hell.
I am thankful for my family being there,
sometimes not, but... Oh, well.

I'm locked up in a jail cell.
When I was little I wrote in a notebook
everything I've been through.
I was born in a refugee camp in Kenya.
The twins, my brother and sister,
they both died in my parents' arms,
starving to eat something,
but they knew it was too late.

On August 28, 2014, I almost died.
Driving out of control, I crashed my father's car,
and I was disgraced in my father's eyes.

I'm locked up in a jail cell.
I feel like I've been to hell and back.
Now I'm thinking to myself, am I ever gonna get out?
I once had a dream this struggle would come to a stop.
I'd feel free, like a bird heading home to his nest,
home to his children.

Fighting with IF

IF is a word I learned to despise
IF is a word that brings tears to my eyes
Trapped within the walls of this cold, stone cell
I relive my past and on it I dwell
In the past IF I had been much wiser
Instead of such a fool
I could have harnessed IF and used it as a tool
In the past IF helped me and guided me with my plans
Now it only mocks as life slips from my hands
I fight with IF all night and day
Wanting to change the past but finding no way
IF is a word I hope to forget
Since it only reminds me of all that I regret

Clarity, Happiness & Love

I am addicted to wanting to be loved,
to be held by someone.
It feels like you're wanted
and you're needed.
It feels like the warmth
of the sun on your skin in the morning.

I am addicted to filling up the empty space in my heart.
I fill it with drugs or sex or liquor.
Even though I know it's not the best thing,
I still try to fill up that empty space in my heart,
like a new house I just moved into.

I am addicted to feeling clarity,
to be sure of myself and the things around,
like a small child who's seen her mother for the first time,
like a child who knows its Mom
because the child grew up within her.
The child loves her mother
no matter if her mother is in her life or not.
I know this because I don't know my mother,
but I know she's mine and I'm hers.

I am addicted to blaming others for my pain,
for the loss of my life, and for not having my mother.
I feel anger and hurt when I blame others.
I blame my stepfather.
I blamed God.

But I am also addicted to not giving up.
Even when I felt worthless,
I never cut my wrists when I wanted to
because I knew that God had something planned for me.
I take each day step by step
like most people do,
walking to happiness
and clarity and love.

———

Dedicated to my mom. I love you.

I'm a Diamond

I'm a diamond
That shines with personality
I'm a diamond
Whose rough edges tell a story of struggle

I live a double life
One full of "the game"
And in the game
They call me
Diamond

I'm a soldier
Whose glare dares you to try
I'm a soldier
Whose glare could numb your insides

I sleep with one eye open
Because a soldier is always ready for a fight

I'm an actor
So good you'll cry
As if it were you dancing with the devil

I'm a magician
Making you the shoes on my feet
The shoes that get mistreated
But pick up their own personal feet
And carry me away

I'm a magician
Making you the eyes on my face
As you scream to look away

I am smart
I am beautiful
I am me

I have struggled
I have a drug problem

I have let life win over me
But no more

I'm going to laugh in life's face and take control
It's my time
I'm grown

For You

In my ocean you are coral
because in my head you are the moral of the story
I can't explain.

In my grassy field you are a dragonfly
because you've earned your wings to me.

In my galaxy you are The Milky Way—
an amusement to the human eye.

In my veins you are a pulse
that keeps the existence of my heart.

How I'm Feeling

I don't know how to explain how I'm feeling—
It's like a warm bowl of noodles
Like Chuck Taylors on my feet, low
Like the smell of a cement garage
Like a stack of bills
Like a hug from a friend after a long time apart
Like sinking into a big pillow

I get to go back to treatment
It means that I'll get another chance
To get my life on track
So I can spend Christmas with my mom and sister

The Missing Puzzle Piece

The girl with the scars—
That's what people call me.

I've always been the type of person to hide everything.
The girl that you'll see with the fat smile,
But the second you turn, I'm crying fat tears.

I don't want to show weakness,
And in my eyes, weakness is crying.
I know it's not true, but I beat myself up over it.

Hyper and upbeat—
In a large group, I'm the one sitting on the wall in silence.

Half the time I'm pretty, half the time I'm ugly.
That's the way I see myself,
And the way others see me, too.

It makes me feel left out,
Like I'm that missing puzzle piece
Stuffed in the back of the closet,
That no one will ever find again.

It's easy to complete a puzzle
With only one piece missing,
But you can't make a puzzle
Out of only one piece.

CPSIA information can be obtained
at www.ICGtesting.com
Printed in the USA
FSOW02n1434020317
31286FS